A Square Peg in a Circular World
A Series of Poems About Social Anxiety

Lori Spensieri

Dedication

The Book is Dedicated to my family and friends who were able to see the real me, beyond my mask of anxiety and depression. Thank you for the love and support.

"Be yourself. Everyone else is already taken."
Oscar Wilde

Table Of Contents

Introduction

She was my best friend. This statement rang true beginning first grade and lasting until the end of eighth. She was not the easiest person to have as a friend. She did not get along with everyone. She was also very demanding. This is the type of person I tend to attract. The reason for this is simple, although the reason was not clear to me for a long time. Growing up I was often told that I am too quiet. I was told that I am too shy. I was told that I am too timid and lastly, I was told that I am too reserved. Harsh judgment was 'offered' from all angles. The truth is, well I was perhaps all of those things, but most of all, I was way too aware of what people may or may not have been thinking of me in any given situation or moment.

I know I was liked and likeable. I just preferred to sit back and take things in. This was often mistaken for snobbishness, coldness or sheer rudeness. Anyone that really knows me knows that I am not rude. I am quite the opposite. I am a sweet, kind, and generous person. I can attest to this. Well, my mom told me so.

Anyway, I can say that my kindness, sweetness and gentleness have not always paid off. These traits have many times been mistaken for weakness or even fearfulness. At my current age, I can proudly say that I care not what people think of me any longer. Just because someone believes something about you, does not make it so. I have found that often when someone makes a harsh judgment of another; it is simply a reflection of his or her own low self-esteem. It has taken me a long time to get here. But here I am.

"You are so weird!" Said Susan.

We were all at Susan's perfectly tidy house. It was in 1989. We were a bunch of 10-year-old sixth graders. We thought we were cool and we thought we knew everything. In hindsight, we were not cool and we knew very little.

This group included Susan, my beautiful, long-haired, perfect, Trinidadian best friend. She was very demanding and she was always right. She was nice but she had a definite mean streak. She wanted what she wanted. She usually got her own way. She was Daddy's princess. Her mean streak showed up in the creation of the "I Hate Lori Club". It was created in response to be declining to attend a fishing trip with her and her dad. The trip sounded, well, horrible. This club was created, and destroyed, in third grade, but I did not forget about it for some time.

These girls and I were having a sleep over at Susan's house, on this particular evening. It was fun up until that moment.

"Why am I weird? She said I was weird," I thought to myself for a good long while. That really resonated with me. The seed was planted. Why am I weird? What did she mean?

Well, truth be told, I am very different from many other people that I have met during my 39 years here on the beautiful green Earth. For starters, my sense of humour is quite different from other females. Farts, burps and bowel movements, in the right context, can be absolutely hilarious. I do laugh profusely while witnessing someone "failing" at life. This could involve; someone falling on ice, flipping backwards while attempting a dangerous twerking stunt (while trying to be sexy), or even when a little kid is dragged along while trying to walk his or her gigantic dog. Those are hilarious, given that no one actually gets hurt. This likely comes from the angelic voice in my head that always forces me to see the good in any situation. I am also different in other ways. I was always very careful and conscientious. I was a perfectionist. I have no competitive bones in my entire body. I have always hated going to parties. I digress again.

As time went on, I made different friends. Susan did not follow the rest of the grade 8 graduating class. I had a new chance to be anyone that I wanted to be upon entering my new school. A new school meant a new beginning.

Enter Donna.

A "Susan" by another name, is still a Susan. She was tall, beautiful and she commanded attention.

As I mentioned before, I attract this type. Tall, skinny, beautiful, demanding, self-assured and, well, perfect. I would always end up being the "D.A.S.H." (Designated, Adorable, Short, Home-girl). I made up this term and I don't expect it to get picked up by popular culture, but it works. Donna was my best friend. She was my best friend until she wasn't. When she decided that I no longer qualified as "BFF" material, I went through my very first existential crisis. It was midway through eleventh grade.

This was when my social anxiety reared its horribly disfigured and hideous face. I started to wonder if people liked me. I started to believe that I had very little to offer in any social situation.

It didn't matter if it was a party, a meeting, a lunch, a baby shower, or the prom. I completely believed that I was broken. I was broken, on a social level anyway. These delusions persisted. They persisted for a long time. As the Law of Attraction says, "What you resist persists." Truer words were never uttered.

Delusions of Persecution

Delusions don't feel like illusions,
They lead to confusion.
It's an ultimate deflation,
Of self-esteem and elation.

These delusions of persecution,
They are part of my imagination.
Although reality is the implication,
From my mind is the ultimate creation.

Alone in a Crowd

Alone in a crowd,
Surrounded by faces.
A sea of smiles,
Small groups of people talking.
About what...? Really.

Why doesn't anyone talk to me?
Am I not enough?
Am I really less than the others?
Am I different? I guess I am.

Alone despite these people,
They don't know I'm here.
Starting today, I make this vow,
I will start to face this fear.

Unicorn at a Horse Party

I clip clop slowly, looking all around.
My horseshoes rhythmically tap the ground.
I am very different.
Oh why did I come?
I reach for my invite,
But I still feel numb.

Horses here, horses there,
Horses, horses, everywhere.
My eyes dart left, my eyes dart right,
I am so alone. It's just not fair.

The only one here that has a horn,
Right at the top of my head.
The only unicorn in the crowd,
My cheeks are turning red.

I do not fit in,
I never will.
They keep staring at my horn.
It used to bring me such intense pride,
This is the way I was born.

A unicorn at the horse party.
Who will be my friend?
They don't see that I am special,
In, I cannot blend.

Perhaps I too am a unicorn,
Never really fitting in.
One day my difference will be my strength,
Up high I will hold my chin.

Waiting

Waiting.
Waiting.
Waiting.
For what? You don't really know.
A feeling of waiting.
A sensation of tugging or pulling,
Or
Waiting …
I sigh, taking in a deep long breath,
Thinking too much and…
Waiting.

Project Pretty

I just want to be pretty.
I just need to be liked.
Adolescence is a very touchy time.
Kids can also be so mean.

Braces on my teeth twice,
Eye-patch for the lazy eye.
Colour the hair.
Get rid of that pesky curl,
Go running every day.
Eat as little as I can,
Count each calorie consumed.
100 sit-ups each morning and night.

The thing that makes me different now,
Will be what makes me special one day. I hope.

Distraction

Staying busy is a great way,
To keep one's mind on track.
Doing chores and hobbies and such,
Or driving there and back.

A busy state is what I maintain,
To keep my thoughts compiled.
If I give my mind one inch,
It will surely run a mile.

Busy writing, cleaning, cooking too,
Follow steps with coded hue.
Fill the mind with things to do,
To send delusions adieu.

But in a quiet moment,
When everyone stays still.
I lost myself in life's free gift,
Reality returns with a chill.

Racing thoughts always return,
I will never win.
All I can do is catch myself,
And comfort from within.

One, two trying to find my shoe,
Three, four - heading for the door.
Five, six - personality I can't fix.
Seven, eight - this side I hate.
Nine ten - I feel like this again.

Family

With family there,
Anxiety wanes.
I feel...happy,
An absence of pain.

It's different with them,
I can just be me.
No fake smiles,
Or urges to flee.

There's mom asking questions,
And dad helping out.
Brother sharing a story,
And sister never shouts.

What could it be about this place?
It makes me stay to calm.
Perhaps it's not the place that counts
But the people, especially Mom.

Family is an F word,
But it does not fit the bill.
Keep your members close to you,
And leave they never will.

On a Low

I'm feeling like I'm on a low,
Spirally down like water flows.
Down and down my mind is oh,
Getting worse ...and moving slow.

Great Day

I'm actually having a really great day,
I wish that I knew why.
A genuine crowd surrounds me,
I'm calm with a natural high.

My mood is good. I feel relaxed,
Something to maintain.
Blood pressure down and mind is clear,
Nothing to restrain.

Mindful.
Blissful.
Zenn-ful.
This state is not my norm.

Joyful.
Thoughtful.
Restful.
Heart is feeling warm.

Sometime later, I start feeling odd,
I try again to fit in with the squad,
I turn around, grin and nod,
But inside I pause and pray to God.

Fitting in may never happen,
I don't know why I try.
I listen for my chance to speak,
Which makes me want to cry.

The key to this, is to be myself,
Content to be just me.
Forget about what others think,
This too shall set you free.

A Secret

I've discovered a secret,
I've discovered the truth.
I've discovered a system,
For returning to youth.

It's all in the thinking,
It's all in the mind.
It's all in the ideas,
Of being happy and kind.

It all started Thursday,
I did decide.
Things would be different,
Life *will* be a great ride.

I used a clear picture,
Inside of my head.
Of me being happy,
And Cheerful instead.

I decided to think of,
Only thoughts good.
Of unicorns and lollipops,
Finally I understood.

No more would I dwell,
On things going wrong.
I'd create a good life,
With belief real and strong.

I have written a list,
Of many good tricks.
For bringing on happy,
And making it stick.

There are affirmations,
That I can say.
I can watch a funny series,
And laugh through the day.

Taking a walk,
Can do such a wonder.
After an error,
Or problem or blunder.

Breathing deep,
Filling the lungs.
Brings clarity and calm,
Climb down a few rungs.

Things feel so different,
I'm not sure what is new.
A fresh lease on life,
Gratitude is due.

I know now,
That I do have control.
Keep positive thoughts,
That is the main goal.

"Follow your Bliss and the universe will open doors for you
where there were only walls."

Joseph Campbell (1904 – 1987)

Sitting

Sitting at this workshop,
Surrounded by my peers.
Everyone is chatting,
This bubbles up my fears.

This is the critical moment,
Where I must stop and pause.
To put this into perspective,
Negativity must be the cause.

I am stopping now,
I push bad thoughts aside.
Focus on this job,
This is what I decide.

What am I?

I think I have discovered my truth,
It makes me feel so free.
It's not an 'illness' that plagues my life,
It's my greatest quality.

I did a funny online quiz,
But it really made me think.
It says I am an Earth angel,
As my stomach sinks.

I look into the mirror and stare,
Could this really be a thing?
I fit all the angel qualities,
Minus the floating halo light-ring.

I love to help others,
I go the extra mile.
I look much younger than I am,
Polite is always my style.

I've always been quite different,
Sometimes a little depressed.
Maybe I just miss my home,
In heaven with no stress.

Please don't get me wrong at all,
I love my life on Earth.
I'm grateful for the family I have,
Two sons that I gave birth.

I love who I am and have become,
I would never change these things.
A comfort to know I'm something more,
An angel with hidden wings.

Angels are among us,
And other creatures too.
Look around and open your mind,
You may just be one too.

"If you must doubt something,
doubt your limits."

Bob Proctor

Nothing Rhymes With Happy

I've decided to write a little poem,
About something important to me.
You see, I sense that the world,
Lacks emotionality

I endeavoured to write a poem,
To teach one to feel better.
A poem designed to be read allowed,
Just like an enveloped wax-sealed letter.

A letter written to all the people,
Who live on this green Earth.
For adults, kids and teens alike,
Who may really doubt their worth.

You see, I had a big problem,
When starting to write these lines.
I couldn't conceive a rhyming word,
With happy…what a crime!

An issue to be resolved,
With a single simple change.
I will settle on the word "content",
And put "happiness" out of range.

I don't really want to give up,
I'll never feel content.
A quitter never prospers,
To succeed I am hell-bent.

Cheerful I'd feel if I found such a word,
To rhyme with happy today.
Then I could continue this poem,
With no further annoying delay.

I could continue to tell you
The benefits of this emotion.
Perhaps it is going to be easy,
Now that the wheels are in motion.

Let's begin at the beginning,
The best place to start.
There is *appy* and *bappy* and *crappy*,
I'll add those to my chart.

There is *dappy* and *flappy* and *gappy*,
I don't know what any of those mean.
Kappy, *lappy* and *mappy*,
Oh how silly this must seem.

Nappy, oh that's a word,
It means diaper I believe.
Not what I was looking for,
It's not what I could conceive.

Pappy means dad or grandpa,
Sappy means sickly sweet.
Zappy sounds kind of fun.
And now I feel defeat.

I wanted to talk about happy,
But I'll settle for "content".
It's a similar emotion,
You know what I really meant.

There are other words that I could use,
But they do seem quite right.
Like CALM or FREE or RICH,
None seem as large or bright.

Wait a minute,
Put this on hold.
I want to use my word.
Happy is the way I feel!
I say it loud and bold.

Happy, Slappy, Yappy and Zappy,
Chappy, Flappy, Mappy and Gappy.
Nappy, Pappy, Strappy and Snappy,
I guess there are a lot of words that rhyme with happy!

Pain in my Fingers

A habit I have tried to quit,
I don't want them to see.
Shame is not needed but,
Embarrassment overwhelm me,

Soon I will stop,
This will not go on.
I tell myself all the time.
It is unhealthy, it doesn't look nice
It has no reason or rhyme.

When I was young,
I was part of a troop.
The girls and I,
Brownies was this group.

Inspection time,
Oh how I hated.
Checking my hands,
Stress not understated.

They inspected our uniform.
They inspected our hair.
They inspected our nails.
They see my hands. It's not fair.

What happened to your fingers they would always ask,
I hide my hands in shame.
I try to make up a decent excuse,
But they still react the same.

It hurts and it looks ugly,
A habit I must quit.
There really is no treatment,
But to wear a pair of mitts.

Dermatillomania is what this is called,
There are so many like me.
This is a fact you'd never know,
As mutilation is not nice to see.

Try getting a manicure,
Or talk to a shrink.
Try out hypnosis,
 Suggestions make me think.

Some say, "Don't do that!"
They really don't understand.
I have not chosen,
To tear apart my hand.

People do not get it,
The reason I do this thing.
I simply cannot help it,
Calm feelings, it does bring.

It's a type of Obsessive Compulsiveness,
The anxiety is the first.
The compulsion is the picking,
The pain is the worst.

Bad News

The news is bad again today,
To live here, I am blessed.
Perhaps I should just shut it off,
The world is a giant mess.

If I turn off the news,
I will not know what is abreast.
I like to hear the happy tales,
I can't avoid the rest.

I see a woman on the news,
Condemned for how she's dressed.
Why can't things be equal and fair?
A longing fills my chest.

I want a world that's equal,
Both genders together to rest.
Side by side holding hands,
With equal passion and zest.

A child is forced to work a job,
He should be on a quest.
To find a toy or game he likes,
But I say all of this in gest.

Another natural disaster,
Puts Mother Nature to the test.
Devastation everywhere,
We have it here the best.

It will get better,
It must improve.
Tying to be positive,
There's nothing left to lose.

Perhaps it will happen,
Peace should be stressed.
This outcome is in question,
And I'm definitely not impressed.

25

"Bad times have a scientific value. These are occasions a
good learner would not miss."

Ralph Waldo Emerson

To Be Frank

To be frank is to be honest.
To be frank is to be real.

Never sugar coating.
Anxious thoughts are floating.

To be frank is to be genuine, just and sincere.
To be frank is to be there and lending an ear.

To be frank is to be level when land meets the skies,
To be frank is to be true blue, the colour of his eyes.

To be frank is to be decent, heart on his sleeve.
To be frank is to have doubts when you want to believe.

Trustworthy and real is what he can be.
He knows not his potential. When will he see?

To be frank is to be great it is a gracious man.
To be frank is to be coveted he's part of my ultimate plan.

I have to share what I believe;
Anxiety doesn't have to leave.
It caused me to roll up my emotional sleeve,
Without you I would surely grieve.

To know you is to know me,
There is no other way.
To love you is to face the fear,
That comes with each new day.

I've started to love you,
It will never stop.
You are a perfect illusion,
Never to fade or crop.

Thoughts in my head,
They may swirl around.
But that doesn't mean,
Confusion abounds.

I know one day,
We will be together.
It may take a while,
Like curing fine leather.

Decisions like these,
Cannot be taken lightly.
To change ones whole life,
To be brave and knightly.

"She was powerful.
Not because she wasn't scared
But because she went on so strongly
Despite the fear"

Atticus

"Bestie" Poem Number One

Surrounded by noise,
It is like a plague.
He knows what he wants,
But, he can be quite vague.

To whittle it down,
To something specific.
Would yield something more,
Something prolific.

Alone in a crowd,
He does tend to feel.
He must know I am with him,
In spirit and zeal.

He has a gift,
With nature's beasts.
Love unconditional,
At the very least

He is kind and sweet,
And says the right things.
By helping others,
He is earning his wings.

Suffering silent,
With emotional pain.
With hopes of a purpose,
And maybe a gain.

Heart so big,
And humour to match.
For the right woman,
He is quite the catch.

I wish him the best,
On his journey through life.
To feel happy and calm,
And minimal strife.

As he read this I hope,
It fills him with peace.
He deserve to feel happy,
And worries to cease.

From me to him,
I give nothing but love.
Spanning Earth on the ground,
To the skies up above.

Meeting in person,
We will certainly one day.
Until then my bestie,
Separated we stay.

"Many people will walk in and out of your life, but only true
friends will leave footprints in your heart."

Eleanor Roosevelt

It Hurts

It hurts when someone hurts you.
The one person who you imagined would never hurt you.
The person that you held in high esteem.
The one you hold closest to your heart.
Your heart that now feels broken.

It hurts when someone hurts you.
The one person on which you thought that you could lean.
When everyone else sucks,
And everyone else does suck.
But now there is no one on which to lean.

Who do you trust when you can't trust the one person you thought you could?

Who do you talk to when you cant talk to the one person you could?

No one.

That is when you realize why you are really here to learn.

You are here to learn about solitude.

There is peace in solitude.

There is quiet and peace.

Social Media

Such a fake.
Is anyone real?
If we post on a platform,
Anyone can take or steal;

Put your best foot forward.
They say to smile for the camera.
We take 20 photos from many different angles.
We apply any filter that makes us look younger, prettier,
thinner.

Social Media is a the best version of you,
Social media can make you feel proud.

"Social media is training us to compare our lives, instead of appreciating everything we are. No wonder why everyone is always depressed."

Bill Murray

Embracing the Strange

You are weird!
You are strange!
You are different from the rest.

You are odd!
You are puzzling!
They put me to the test.

It took years and years to stop hearing them.
Years and years to ignore.
Even longer to stop and flip it around,
And stop feeling cuts so sore.

To see myself as different,
It is something to be desired.
To shine brighter than the brightest star,
And stop feeling sick and tired.
One night something happened
An epiphany so real
My eyes suddenly opened
I knew this was a big deal

My differences suddenly seemed so great
No longer a burden
What makes me strange?
Is what makes me strong?
Of this, I was absolutely certain!
If you are quiet…
It is ok!
You don't have to always chime in,
One day when you finally choose to speak
Your words will be so much more powerful

Enough 1

Stop the medication
Enough with conformation
All it takes is a decision
To face your fears with dedication
The next is realization
That you need not meet the world's expectations
The only one you must give satisfaction
Is the person in the mirror's reflection!

"Enough is enough and it is time for a change."

Owen Heart

Enough 2

Enough Anxiety	More Awareness
Enough Bullshit	More Belonging
Enough Comparing	More Caring for others
Enough Dread	More Dreaming
Enough Extinction	More Elation
Enough Fear	More Friendship
Enough Gray	More Gratitude
Enough Hiding	More Hero's
Enough Interference	More Intelligence
Enough Judgment	More Joking around
Enough Killing	More Kisses
Enough Labels	More Love
Enough Male-dominance	More Meaning
Enough Negative self-talk	More Nature
Enough Ostracizing	More Optimism
Enough Physical abuse	More Present
Enough Quietly suffering	More Questions
Enough Rushing	More Reasoning
Enough Sadness	More Sharing
Enough Tears	More Time
Enough Ugliness	More Understanding
Enough Violence	More Victory
Enough Wandering	More Wandering
Enough X-plaining	More X-citing
Enough Yelling	More Yearning
Enough Zeros	More Zeal

Keep a Go

Before my Nonna passed away,
She told us one last thing.
She said no matter what happens,
You should always dance and sing.

Life is short and troubles loom,
Things are not always fair.
But, if you stop and look at life,
You have the skills to bear.

"Keep a go," Nonna would say,
It meant to stand not sit.
At times when life gives lemons,
Make lemonade, don't quit.

She is gone but her message remains,
Never dwell on the bad.
The world is full and awesome and good,
So smile friend, don't be sad.

Compare as we Dare

Who has the best hair?
Whose skin is more fare?
Whose ass is shaped like a pear?

Whose eyes are more rare?
Who's styled with more flare?
Who acts with more love and more care?

Who deserves the most air?
Who gets a fair share?
Compare, compare as we dare!

People

Some people are happy,
And some are not.
Some don't know why,
Some reasons are sought.

Situation, relation or even the season,
Sometimes there is no actual reason.

There is one thing that we must all do,
If some form of happiness will ever ensue.

Love yourself and love one another,
Friend or foe, sister or brother.

I have learned to finally love myself,
And put reservations.
My face, my hair,
My nose and skin fair.

My body is perfect.
My heart beating fast.
My mind is unique.

"I would rather walk with a friend
in the dark, than alone in the light."

Helen Keller

Conclusion

We are all special in our own little way. The trick is to see that special quality or difference in you. Find it. See it as a bonus. This difference is a benefit to you. One day, this special quality will cease to feel like a burden. It will be the thing that sets you apart from the masses.

It will be your strength. Nurture it

Contact Informaiton

Our Email Address

ehbepositive@gmail.com

Our Website and Blog

www.ehbepositive.com

Find us on Facebook

Join our Group called "Eh! Be Positive"
https://www.facebook.com/groups/ehbepositive/

Join our Page called "Eh! Be Positive"
https://www.facebook.com/ehbepositive/

Find us on YouTube

Subscribe to our channel
Eh! Be Positive

https://www.youtube.com/channel/UCyrjfWz_CVGlzVToI
pcEiNg

Find us on Twitter
Eh, Be Positive
Or tweet us @spensierimethod

Find us on Instragram by adding us at *ehbepositive.*
Or go to
https://www.instagram.com/ehbepositive/

Find us on Pinterest by following us at
https://www.pinterest.ca/thirtydaystoaha/pins/

Thank you for reading my book.

To all of my supporters, family and friends alike, thank
you for supporting me in my endeavors, no matter now
big or small.

Other Titles By Lori Spensieri

"10 Ways to Happy"

"A performance based technique to finding happiness in one's life.

Each of the 10 ways to happy are fully explained, with examples. You will find your way to a happier life with the help of this book and our social media supports. "

"*30 Days to a Happier You*" By Lori Spensieri and Cara Spensieri

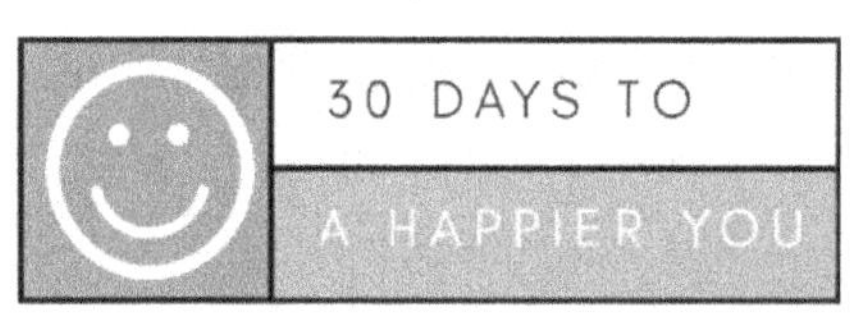